MW01242585

KNOWING JESUS

THROUGH THE LAW AND THE PROPHETS

Messianic Prophecies Study Guide

by Juli Camarin

ISBN-13: 978-0615845289
ISBN-10: 0615845282

Project Editors: Dave Seawel, Sue Bussey

Cover Art by Juli Camarin.

Special Thanks to Greg Fritz Ministries and his teaching on "The Ministry of Jesus"

Contents

Knowing Jesus Through the Law and the Prophets

There can be NO DOUBT that Jesus is the Messiah. For the believer; it is important to understand for ourselves that He is the promised Christ. Jesus showed us how important this was on the Road to Emmaus; when revealing himself to the men as they walked; He explained who He was through the law and prophets. "He said to them; "How foolish you are; and how slow of heart to believe all that the prophets have spoken! Did not the Christ have to suffer these things and then enter his glory?" **And beginning with Moses and all the Prophets; he explained to them what was said in all the Scriptures concerning himself"** (Luke 24:25-27).

Jesus proved who He was by the scriptures; this is why it is imperative; as believers to understand these things; so it solidifies who Jesus is as the foundation of our faith. In the Bible there are over 60 major prophecies; Jesus fulfilled them all. The mathematical probability would be impossible for anyone else to have fulfilled even a fraction of these IF he wasn't the Messiah. **By studying these things; it   proves without a shadow of a doubt that Jesus is the long awaited Savior! This good news!**

Here is complied a list of some of these prophecies and either noted or referenced how Jesus or others fulfilled them. This is meant; not as a definitive list; but rather to be used as a tool for further study. **Enjoy!**

"He said to them; "This is what I told you while I was still with you: **Everything must be fulfilled that is written about me in the Law of Moses; the Prophets and the Psalms.**" Then he opened their minds **so they could understand the Scriptures**" (Luke 24:44-45).

***Special Notes:**

These Old Testament prophecies took place 500 to 1;200 years before Jesus' birth.

Not only did Jesus fulfill these prophecies but many prophecies were fulfilled by others which adds to the mathematical improbability if Jesus wasn't the Christ.

Notes

Messianic Prophecies About Jesus' Lineage

Son of God
Prophesied in Psalm 2:7
Fulfilled in Matthew 3:17; 8:29; 16:16; Mark 1:11;
Luke 1:32;35; Acts 13:33; Hebrews 1:5; 5:5;
II Peter 1:17

Firstborn Over All Creation
Prophesied in Psalm 89:27
Fulfilled in Romans 8:29; Colossians 1:15

First Born Son; Sanctified and Consecrated to the Lord
Prophesied in Exodus 13:2; Numbers 3:13; 8:17
Fulfilled in Luke 2:7; 23

Born of the Seed of Abraham
Prophesied in Genesis 17:7-8; 26:3-4
Fulfilled in Matthew 1:1; 17; Galatians 3:16; 29;
Hebrews 2:16

Born of the Seed of Isaac
Prophesied in Genesis 17:19; 21:12; 26:2-4
Fulfilled in Matthew 1:2; 17; Romans 9:7;
Hebrews 11:17-19

Born of the Seed of Jacob
Prophesied in Genesis 28:13-14; Numbers 24:17-19
Fulfilled in Matthew 1:2; Luke 1:33; 3:23-38

Notes

Seed of David
Prophesied in Psalm 89:3-4
Fulfilled in John 7:42; Acts 13:22-23

From the Tribe of Judah
Prophesied in Genesis 49:8-10; Micah 5:2
Fulfilled in Matthew 1:1-3; Hebrews 7:14; Revelation 5:5

Branch From the Root of Jesse
Prophesied in Isaiah 11:1-2
Fulfilled in Matthew 1:6; Acts 13:22-23

Born of David's Royal Line
Prophesied in Isaiah 9:7; II Samuel 7:12-13;
Jeremiah 23:5; 30:9
Fulfilled in Matthew 1:1; Luke 1:32; Acts 13:22-23

Notes

Messianic Prophecies About Jesus' Birth

Born of a Virgin
Prophesied in Isaiah 7:13-14
Fulfilled in Matthew 1:18-23; Luke 1:26-35

Immanuel; God with Us
Prophesied in Isaiah 7:14; 8:8;10
Fulfilled in Matthew 1:21-23; John 1:14; 14:8-11;
Colossians 2:9

God's Son Would Be Given
Prophesied in Isaiah 9:6
Fulfilled in John 3:16; Romans 8:32

Messiah Comes from Bethlehem
Prophesied in Micah 5:2
Fulfilled in Matthew 2:1; 5-6; Luke 2:4-7

Kings Would Bring Gifts
Prophesied in Psalm 72:10-11
Fulfilled in Matthew 2:1-11

Children Would Be Killed in Bethlehem
Prophesied in Jeremiah 31:15
Fulfilled in Matthew 2:16-18

Was Called Out of Egypt
Prophesied in Hosea 11:1
Fulfilled in Matthew 2:13-15; 19-21

Notes

Messianic Prophecies About Jesus' Life

Messenger Sent to Announce Him
Prophesied in Isaiah 40:3-5
Fulfilled Matthew 3:3; Mark 1:3; Luke 3:3-5; John 1:23
Prophesied in Malachi 3:1
Fulfilled in Matthew 11:10; Mark 1:2-4; 7; Luke 7:27-28
Prophesied in Malachi 4:5-6
Fulfilled in Matthew 11:13-14; Mark 9:11-13;
Luke 1:17; 7:27-28

The Spirit of the Lord Would Rest on Him
Prophesied in Isaiah 11:2; 42:1; 61:1-2
Fulfilled in Matthew 3:16; Mark 1:10; Luke 3:22; 4:18;
John 1:32; 3:34; Acts 10:38

Anointed to Preach Liberty to the Captives
Prophesied in Isaiah 61:1-2
Fulfilled in Luke 4:16-21; Acts 10:38

God Would Dwell With His People
Prophesied in Zechariah 2:10-13
Fulfilled in John 1:14; Revelation 21:3

Settles in Capernaum
Prophesied in Isaiah 9:1-2
Fulfilled in Matthew 4:12-16; Luke 4:31-31
(The great light in Galilee was Jesus and the land of
Zebulun and Naphtali was Galilee)

Notes

"I AM"
Prophesied in Exodus 3:13-15
Fulfilled in John 8:24; 13:19

Be Sinless
Prophesied in Isaiah 53:9
Fulfilled in I Peter 2:22

Call Those Who Were Not His People
Prophesied in Isaiah 55:4-5; Hosea 2:23
Fulfilled in Romans 9:23-26

Stumbling Stone to the Jews
Prophesied in Isaiah 8:14
Fulfilled in Romans 9:31-33; I Peter 2:7-8

Heal the Deaf and the Blind
Prophesied in Isaiah 29:18; Isaiah 35:5
Fulfilled in Matthew 11:5; Mark 7:37;
Luke 7:19-22; John 9:39

Light to the Gentiles
Prophesied in Isaiah 42:6; 49:6
Fulfilled in Luke 2:25-32; Acts 26:23

Prophet Like Moses
Prophesied in Deuteronomy 18:15;18;19
Fulfilled in Matthew 21:11; Luke 7:16; 24:19;
John 6:14; 7:40; Acts 3:18-22

Hated without Reason
Prophesied in Psalm 35:19; 69:4
Fulfilled in John 15:24-25

Notes

Come To Do the Will of God
Prophesied in Psalm 40:7-8
Fulfilled in Matthew 26:39; Hebrews 10:5-9

Delights to Do God's Will
Prophesied in Psalm 40:8
Fulfilled in John 4:34; 6:38

Anointed By God
Prophesied in Psalm 45:6-7
Fulfilled in Hebrews 1:8-9

Have Zeal For God's House
Prophesied in Psalm 69:9
Fulfilled in John 2:17

Care for the Poor and Needy
Prophesied in Psalm 72:12-14
Fulfilled in Luke 7:22

Speak in Parables
Prophesied in Psalm 78:2
Fulfilled in Matthew 13:10-16; 34;35; Luke 8:10

Pray For His Enemies
Prophesied in Psalm 109:4
Fulfilled in Matthew 5:44; Luke 23:34

Heal and Do Miracles
Prophesied in Isaiah 35:4-6
Fulfilled in Matthew 9:30; 11:4-6; 12:22; 20:34;
21:14; Mark 7:32-35; Acts 10:38

Notes

Shepard Who Tends His Sheep
Prophesied in Isaiah 40:10-11
Fulfilled in John 10:11; Hebrews 13:20; I Peter 2:25

God's Servant
Prophesied in Isaiah 42:1-4
Fulfilled in Matthew 12:16-21

Redeemer to Come Out of Zion
Prophesied in Isaiah 59:16-20
Fulfilled in Romans 11:26-27

The People's Hearts Would Be Hardened
Prophesied in Isaiah 6:9-10
Fulfilled in Matthew 13:13-15; John 12:37-40;
Acts 28:24-27

Notes

Messianic Prophecies about Jesus' Crucifixion

The King Comes Riding On a Donkey
Prophesied in Zechariah 9:9
Fulfilled in Matthew 21:1-5; Mark 11:1-10;
Luke 19:28-38; John 12:14-15.

Betrayed by a Close Friend
Prophesied in Psalm 41:9; Psalm 55:12-14
Fulfilled in Matthew 26:14-16; 23; 47-50;
Luke 22:19-23; 48; John 13:18-30; 18:2-5

Betrayed by a Kiss
Prophesied in Psalm 41:9; Psalm 55:12-14
Fulfilled in Matthew 26:48; Mark 14:44-45;
Luke 22:47-48

Jesus Was Betrayed By 30 Pieces of Silver
Prophesied in Zechariah 11:12
Fulfilled in Matthew 26:15

Blood Money Was Used To Buy the Potters Field
Prophesied in Zechariah 11:13
Fulfilled in Matthew 27:3-10; referred to in Acts 1:16-19

Beaten and Spit On
Prophesied in Isaiah 50:6
Fulfilled in Matthew 26:67; 27:26-30; Mark 14:65;
15:15-19; Luke 22:63-65; John 19:1

Notes

Forsaken By God
Prophesied in Psalm 22:1
Fulfilled in Matthew 27:46; Mark 15:34

Ridiculed
Prophesied in Psalm 22:7; 17
Fulfilled in Matthew 27:29; 40-44; Mark 15:29-32;
Luke 23:35-39

Rejected By His Brothers
Prophesied in Psalm 69:8
Fulfilled in John 7:3-5

Rulers Rose Up Against Him
Prophesied in Psalm 2:1-2
Fulfilled in Matthew 12:14; 26:3-4; 47; Luke 23:11-2

Rejected as Capstone
Prophesied in Psalm 118:22-23;
Fulfilled in Matthew 21:42; Acts 4:9-12; I Peter 2:6-8

The Passover Lamb with No Broken Bones
Prophesied in Exodus 12:46; Numbers 9:12;
Psalm 34:20
Fulfilled in John 19:31-36

Be Hung on a Tree and Cursed
Prophesied in Deuteronomy 21:23
Fulfilled in Galatians 3:13

Be Thirsty
Prophesied in Psalm 22:15
Fulfilled in John 19:28

Notes

Be Falsely Accused
Prophesied in Psalm 27:12; 35:11
Fulfilled in Matthew 26:60; Mark 14:55-61

Be Struck on the Head
Prophesied in Micah 5:1
Fulfilled in Matthew 27:30

Hands and Feed Pierced
Prophesied in Psalm 22:16; Zechariah 12:10
Fulfilled in Matthew 27:35; John 19:18; 34-37;
John 20:25-29 (Special Note: This was written long
before the practice of crucifixion has been invented)

His Body Would be Pierced
Prophesied in Zechariah 12:10
Fulfilled in John 19:34-37

Cast Lots for Clothing
Prophesied in Psalm 22:18
Fulfilled in Matthew 27:35; Mark 15:24; Luke 23:34;
John 19:23-23

Given Gall and Vinegar to Drink
Prophesied in Psalm 69:20-22
Fulfilled in Matthew 27:34; 48; Mark 15:23; 15:36;
Luke 23:36; John 19:29

Notes

Be Beaten Beyond Recognition

Prophesied in Isaiah 52:14
Fulfilled in Hebrews 5:8; I Peter 2:21

Bore our Griefs and Sorrows

Prophesied in Isaiah 53:4-5
Fulfilled in Matthew 8:17; Romans 5:6-8

Wounded for Our Transgressions

Prophesied in Isaiah 53:5
Fulfilled in I Corinthians 15:3; II Corinthians 5:21;
I Peter 3:18

Lamb Lead To the Slaughter

Prophesied in Isaiah 53:7
Fulfilled in John 1:29;36; Acts 8:28-35; I Peter 1:19;
Revelation 5:6

He Would Be Deserted By His Followers

Prophesied in Zechariah 13:6-7
Fulfilled in Matthew 26:31; 56; Mark 14:27;
John 16:32

Sin Offering

Prophesied in Isaiah 53:10-11
Fulfilled in Acts 10:43; 13:38-39; Romans 3:21-26;
4:5-8; Ephesians 1:7; I Peter 2:21-25; I John 2:2

Sun Would Go Down at Noon

Prophesied in Amos 8:9
Fulfilled in Matthew 27:45; Mark 15:33; Luke 23:44

Notes

Strike the Shepard
Prophesied in Zechariah 13:7
Fulfilled in Mark 14:27

Despised and Rejected
Prophesied in Isaiah 53:2-3
Fulfilled in Matthew 26:67; Luke 17:25;
Luke 23:18; John 1:11

Accused But Did Not Open His Mouth
Prophesied in Isaiah 53:7
Fulfilled in Matthew 26:62-63; 27:12;14;
Mark 14:61; 15:5; Luke 23:9; John 19:9

Numbered/Crucified with the Transgressors
Prophesied in Isaiah 53:12
Fulfilled in Matthew 27:38; Mark 15:27-28;
Luke 22:37; 23:32-33

Spotless Passover Lamb; Slain
Prophesied in Exodus 12:1-11; Isaiah 53:7
Fulfilled in John 1:29-36; I Corinthians 5:7-8;
I Peter 1:18-19; Revelation 5:6-13; 7:14;
21:22-27; 22:1-4

Be Lifted Up as Moses Lifted the Serpent
Prophesied in Numbers 21:8-9
Fulfilled in John 3:14-15

Reproach of Others Fall on Him
Prophesied in Psalm 69:9
Fulfilled in Romans 15:3

Notes

Commit His Spirit into God's Hand
Prophesied in Psalm 31:5
Fulfilled in Luke 23:46

Buried with the Rich
Prophesied in Isaiah 53:9
Fulfilled in Matthew 27:57-60

Swallow Up Death in Victory
Prophesied in Isaiah 25:8
Fulfilled in I Corinthians 15:54-57

Special Note:
Isaiah 53 gives more information about what Jesus was doing behind the scenes than Matthew; Mark; Luke and John's eyewitness account. The WHOLE chapter talks about Jesus from beginning to End.

Notes

Prophecies of the Resurrection

Be Raised from the Dead
Prophesied in Psalm 16:8-11
Fulfilled in Luke 24:6-8; John 20;
Acts 1:3; 2:32; 13:34-37; II Timothy 2:8

Conquered Death
Prophesied in Psalm 16:8-11; 49:15; 86:13
Fulfilled in Acts 2:24-36; 13:30-39; I Corinthians 15:3-4

Ascended on High
Prophesied in Psalm 68:18
Fulfilled in Luke 24:51; Acts 1:9; Ephesians 4:8

Veil Torn in Two
Prophesied in Exodus 26:31-35
Fulfilled in Matthew 27:51; Mark 15:38;
Hebrews 10:19-20

Usher in a New Covenant
Prophesied in Jeremiah 31:31-34; 32:37-40; 50:5
Fulfilled in Matthew 26:27-29; Mark 14:22-24;
Luke 22:15-20; I Corinthians 11:25; Hebrews 8:8-12;
10:15-20

Have Eternal Existence
Prophesied in Micah 5:2
Fulfilled in John 1:1; 4; 8:58; Colossians 1:15-19;
Hebrews 7:23-25

Notes

Establish A New Priesthood
Prophesied in Zechariah 3:8
Fulfilled in Hebrews 7:11-18; I Peter 2:5;9;
Revelation 1:6; 5:10

Be High Priest
Prophesied in Zechariah 6:12-13
Fulfilled in Hebrews 7:11-28; 8:1-2

Be a High Priest Like Melchizedek
Prophesied in Psalm 110:4
Fulfilled in Hebrews 5:1-6; 6:20; 7:15-17

Government Would Be on His Shoulders
Prophesied in Isaiah 9:6
Fulfilled in Matthew 28:18; I Corinthians 15:24-25

Everlasting and Unchanging
Prophesied in Psalm 102:24-27
Fulfilled in Hebrews 1:10-12; 13:8

Restore David's House
Prophesied in Amos 9:11-12
Fulfilled in Acts 15:16-18

David's Lord Seated at God's Right Hand
Prophesied in Psalm 110:1
Fulfilled in Matthew 22:41-45; Mark 12:35-37;
16:19; Acts 7:56

Notes

The Holy Spirit Would Be Poured Out On People
Prophesied in Joel 2:28-32
Fulfilled in Acts 2:16-23

Special Note:
Matthew 27:52 records the resurrection of holy people immediately after Jesus' death proving that death was defeated and the cross was a COMPLETE VICTORY!

Notes

General Messianic Prophecies About Jesus

Women's Offspring Will Crush the Serpents Head
Prophesied in Genesis 3:14-15
Fulfilled in Galatians 4:4; Hebrews 2:14; I John 3:8

All Nations Would Be Blessed Through Abraham
Prophesied in Genesis 12:3; 18:17-18; 22:18;
26:4; 28:14;
Fulfilled in Acts 3:25-26; Galatians 3:16

A Nazarene
Prophesied in Isaiah 4:2; 11:1
Fulfilled in Matthew 2:23; Revelation 5:5; 22:16
(Nazarene means Branch; Separate One)

Chief Cornerstone
Prophesied in Psalm 118:22-23
Fulfilled in Matthew 21:42; Mark 12:10-11; Luke 20:17;
Acts 4:10-12; Ephesians 2:20; I Peter 2:4-7

A Prophet Like Moses
Prophesied in Deuteronomy 18:18-19
Fulfilled in John 1:21; 6:14; Acts 3:22-23; Hebrews 3:1-6

The Throne of David Would Be Forever
Prophesied in II Samuel 7:12-13;16;25-26; Psalm 89:3-4;
36-37; Isaiah 9:7; I Chronicles 17:11-14; 23-27
Fulfilled in Luke 1:32-33; Acts 2:29-26; II Timothy 2:8;
Hebrews 1:8

Notes

Promised Redeemer
Prophesied in Job 19:25-27; Psalm 130:7-8; Isaiah 59:20
Fulfilled in Galatians 4:4-5; Titus 2:13-14

King of Righteousness
Prophesied in Psalm 40:8; Psalm 45:6;7
Fulfilled in Hebrews 1:8-9

A Stumbling Block
Prophesied in Isaiah 8:14-15
Fulfilled in Matthew 21:42-44; Romans 9:32-33;
I Peter 2:6-8

A Light Shining Out of the Darkness
Prophesied in Isaiah 9:1-2
Fulfilled in Matthew 4:14-16; Luke 1:7-9; 2:32;
John 1:4-5

Prince of Peace
Prophesied in Isaiah 9:6
Fulfilled in John 14:27; Acts 10:36; Romans 5:1;
Ephesians 2:14; Colossians 1:20

A Sure Foundation
Prophesied in Isaiah 28:16
Fulfilled in Romans 9:33: I Peter 2:6

The Righteous Branch
Prophesied in Jeremiah 23:5-6; 33:15-16
Fulfilled in Romans 3:22; I Corinthians 1:30;
II Corinthians 5:21; Philippians 3:9

Notes

The Good Shepard
Prophesied in Ezekiel 34:23-24; 37:24
Fulfilled in John 10:11; Hebrews 13:20; I Peter 2:25

Another to Succeed Judas
Prophesied in Psalm 109:7-8
Fulfilled in Acts 1:16-20; Acts 13:2-3

Notes

Prophecies About Jesus' Return

Son of Man Coming in the Clouds

"In my vision at night I looked; and there before me was one like a son of man; coming with the clouds of heaven. He approached the Ancient of Days and was led into his presence. He was given authority; glory and sovereign power; all peoples; nations and men of every language worshiped him. His dominion is an everlasting dominion that will not pass away; and his kingdom is one that will never be destroyed" (Daniel 7:13-15).

They Will Look On The One They Pierced

"And I will pour out on the house of David and the inhabitants of Jerusalem a spirit of grace and supplication. They will look on me; the one they have pierced; and they will mourn for him as one mourns for an only child; and grieve bitterly for him as one grieves for a firstborn son" (Zechariah 12:10).

It will be a Damascus road experience for the whole Jewish nation (Look at Romans 11)

What Are These Wounds On Your Hands?

"If someone asks him; 'What are these wounds on your body?' he will answer; 'The wounds I was given at the house of my friends'" (Zechariah 13:6).

A Nation Will Be Born in a Day

Prophesied in Isaiah 66. This is the Jews after the see the second coming of Chris

Notes

Interesting Observations

Jesus Preached Through the Old Testament Scriptures

Paul said in Romans; "Now to him who is able to establish you by my gospel and the **proclamation of Jesus Christ; according to the revelation of the mystery hidden for long ages past; but now revealed and made known through the prophetic writings** by the command of the eternal God; so that all nations might believe and obey him— to the only wise God be glory forever through Jesus Christ! Amen" (Romans 16:25-27). The gospel was a mystery from the world beginning; but **it is made manifest through preaching the prophecy about Jesus.** It was a mystery and kept secret; but now **we can preach Jesus through the Old Testament scriptures about Him**...incredible!

Wisdom of the Age Comes to Nothing!

The rulers of this age wisdom comes to nothing (I Corinthians 2:6). This wisdom has nothing to do with Jesus' death; resurrection and lordship. God's hidden wisdom was planned before the ages for our glory (I Corinthians 2:7). **If the rulers knew this they would not have crucified the Lord of Glory** (I Corinthians 2:8). Death will never be the same again. The devil did the lag work; Jesus had the victory!

Notes

About Juli

Juli has been writing since a young age. The practice of journaling scriptural insights started during her sophomore year in high school as quiet time devotions. Since then, this habit of studying and writing on the scriptures has become a lifelong learning journey.

Juli currently blogs at JCBlog.net, a blog dedicated to exploring God's Word and planting the seeds of life. The internet has been a wonderful platform to share the good news of the gospel of Jesus Christ and her blog is well-read throughout the world.

Juli currently lives in Iowa with her husband. Read more about her at jcblog.net/juli-camarin.

This book, and others like it are available online at jcblog.net/books or by scanning the QR code.

Made in the USA
Middletown, DE
05 December 2022

17154883R00029